In this book, Ben, Jo, Danny and Amber want to solve some science puzzles. They all have different ideas. Can you help them answer their questions?

What do YOU think about our ideas? Do you have any other ideas? Why don't you talk to someone about what you think?

We'll show you how we try to find out the answers. You can try to find out too!

Ben

Jo

A note to adults ▶

This book shows children that science is everywhere, and that they can find out about the world for themselves by thinking and investigating.

You can help children by reading the book with them and asking questions. At the start of each story, talk about what the characters are saying. While children are investigating, you could ask: What is happening? What can you see? Why do you think this is happening? Is it what you expected to happen? Children should be supervised while they are doing the investigations.

Each story ends with a simple explanation of what has happened. There are ideas for follow-up activities at the back of the book, and children may also want to find out more from other books, CD-Roms or the Internet.

Text copyright © 2000 Brenda and Stuart Naylor
Illustrations copyright © 2000 Ged Mitchell

Designed by Sarah Borny
Edited by Anne Clark

The rights of Brenda and Stuart Naylor and Ged Mitchell to be identified
as the authors and artist of this work have been asserted.

First published in 2000 by Hodder Children's Books,
a division of Hodder Headline,
338 Euston Road, London NW1 3BH

ISBN 0340 76442 2 Hardback
ISBN 0340 76443 0 Paperback
Printed in Hong Kong

The Seesaw
and other science questions ▶

**Brenda and
Stuart Naylor**

Illustrated by
Ged Mitchell

*Hodder
Children's
Books*

a division of Hodder Headline

The Seesaw

Jo, Ben and Amber are at the playground. Ben and Jo are on the seesaw. Ben is bigger than Jo, and the seesaw won't balance.

**Danny will help
you investigate.**

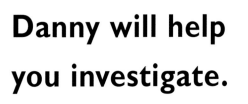 Make a seesaw from
a ruler and a rubber.
Balance the ruler on
the rubber.

2 Put six coins in a
pile on one side and
three of the same
coins on the other.

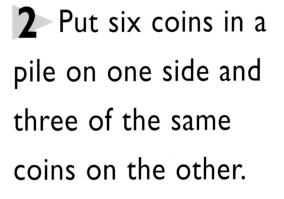

3 Try the coins in different places on the ruler.

4 See how they balance best.

What did you find out?

Big children and smaller children can use a seesaw together. It all depends on where they sit. The big child needs to be nearer the middle to make it balance. The smaller child needs to be further from the middle.

**Amber will help
you investigate.**

Fasten a cotton
handkerchief over a
small bowl or cup.

Pour a big spoonful of
water on to the cotton.

Do the same thing
with a small plastic bag

▶ Now do the same thing with a woolly sock.

▶ Leave them for a while. See which one lets the least water through.

What did you find out? ▶

Some things keep out water better than others. We say that they are waterproof. Plastic is usually waterproof because it doesn't have tiny holes in it like cotton or wool.

Time for Tea

Amber, Ben and Danny are washing up the mugs after tea. There is sugar left at the bottom of the mugs.

There's still sugar in the mugs. We can't have stirred the tea.

**Jo will help
you investigate.**

▶ Find three mugs
and some sugar. You
can see brown sugar
better than white.

2▶ Put one spoon of
sugar in a mug of cold
water and
stir it.

3▶ Put one spoon of
sugar in a mug of
warm water.
Don't stir it.

4 Put one spoon of sugar in a mug of warm water and stir it.

5 Wait a while and see if any sugar is left in the bottom of the mugs.

What did you find out?

Sugar and salt can mix so well with water that you can't see them any more. We call this dissolving. They mix best with water when it is warm and stirred.

Ben will help you investigate.

▌► Find a piece of shiny aluminium foil and a torch.

2► Take the foil into a very dark room or cupboard. How well can you see it?

3 Switch on the torch. How well does the foil shine now?

4 When does the foil show up best?

What did you find out?

Now you have started finding out, you might not want to stop!

The Seesaw

What if you have three people on the seesaw? Where would they sit? What if the dog sat on someone's knee? Would someone have to move?

A Rainy Day

What other fabrics would be good for a rainhat? What about net curtain, velvet or nylon? Sometimes things appear to be waterproof until you touch them. Try putting water on your fabrics, then touching them.

Time for Tea

Try mixing other things with water. You could try flour, sand, coffee and custard powder. Do some things dissolve better than others? Can you find anything else that dissolves in water?

The Lost Coin

What else reflects the light? What can you find around your home? Do some things reflect light better than others? What about mirrors, windows and spoons?

Have fun finding out more!